D1605543

A Discovery Biography

Mary Todd Lincoln

— ◆ —

President's Wife

by LaVere Anderson
illustrated by Cary

CHELSEA JUNIORS
A division of Chelsea House Publishers
New York • Philadelphia

With love to Pauline LaVere Thixton

The Discovery Books have been prepared under the
educational supervision of Mary C. Austin, Ed.D.,
Reading Specialist and Professor of Education, Case
Western Reserve University.

Cover illustration: Judith Brown

First Chelsea House edition 1991

Copyright © MCMXCI by Chelsea House Publishers, a division
of Main Line Book Co. All rights reserved. Printed and bound in
the United States of America.
© MCMLXXV by LaVere Anderson

3 5 7 9 8 6 4

ISBN 0-7910-1415-0

Contents

Chapter *1*

Girl of Kentucky

"Lizzie, come look out the window! Hurry!" Mary Todd cried. "There is a man hiding by the back fence."

Her cousin ran to the window. "It's almost too dark to see—," she began. "Oh, you mean that black shadow under the willow tree! Do you suppose he is a robber?"

The two ten-year-olds were in Mary's bedroom in the beautiful Todd home in Lexington, Kentucky. It was a summer evening in 1829. Mary had been born in Lexington on December 13, 1818. Cousin Lizzie Humphreys was visiting the Todds and shared Mary's room.

"Look, there's Mammy Sally going out to him," Mary said. "She's carrying something in a sack."

Lizzie leaned out the open window to see better. "She's giving the sack to him. Why, she's friends with a robber!"

"She is not!" Mary said. Mammy Sally was the kindly black woman who took care of the Todd children. Mary loved her and trusted her. She knew Mammy Sally would not do anything wrong.

The shadow slipped away into the night. Mammy Sally came back across the yard.

"Let's go ask her who the man was," Mary said. She led the way down the stairs to the big kitchen.

Mammy Sally was alone. She looked worried when the girls told her what they had seen.

"Was that a robber?" Lizzie asked.

"He was only a hungry man. I gave him some food," Mammy Sally answered.

"Why didn't he come to the house to eat?" Mary asked. "Ma always feeds anyone who comes. Why was he hiding?"

Mammy Sally looked more worried than ever. At last she said, "Can you girls keep a secret?" The girls nodded.

"He was a runaway slave," Mammy Sally said. "There are a lot of poor black men like him trying to get away from bad slave owners. If they can reach Canada they will be free and safe. I have put a mark on the fence to show I will feed anyone who needs help. Other slaves pass the word to the runaways. After dark every night I keep watch, and when I see someone I go out."

The girls' eyes grew wide. They knew it was dangerous to help runaways. The slaves' masters could make trouble for anyone who did.

Mary threw her arms around her brave old nurse. "We'll never tell," she promised. "I am glad you help the men. I will help too if I can. But Canada is a long way off, isn't it?"

"A long, hard way," Mammy Sally said sadly. "Most of them will be caught before they can get there."

The next morning the girls went to look at the back fence. They found a deep cut Mammy Sally had made in the wood. Near the fence stood the willow tree. Mary walked over to it. Suddenly she said, "These long, thin willow branches are soft enough to bend into hoops. Let's pick some and sew them inside our Sunday dresses. I'm tired of little-girl clothes. Hoop skirts are so pretty."

"We are too young for hoop skirts," Lizzie said. "What will Aunt Betsy say?"

"When she sees how pretty our dresses are—," Mary began. Then she stopped. What *would* her stepmother, Betsy, say? "Ma is always wanting me to be a lady. And hoop skirts are *very* ladylike!"

Mary began to break branches from the tree. Soon Lizzie was helping her. When they had gathered enough, they hurried to their room.

"I'm glad Elizabeth did not see us," Mary said. "She would have asked all sorts of questions."

Elizabeth was Mary's oldest sister. Mary had two other sisters and two brothers. They were the children of Robert Smith Todd and his first wife. Mary's mother had died when Mary was six. Later Mr. Todd had married again. Now he and the second Mrs. Todd had small children.

All that Saturday Mary and Lizzie worked away. By evening their little white skirts swelled from the hoops sewn into them.

"We will wear them to Sunday School tomorrow," Mary said happily.

Sunday morning the girls put on their hoop dresses and went proudly down to breakfast. The family was in the dining room.

"My goodness, just look at Mary and Lizzie!" Elizabeth exclaimed. "Ugh, what a sight!"

Everybody stared. Then some of the children laughed.

"Girls!" Mrs. Todd gasped. "What have you done to your dresses?"

"We've put hoops in them, ma," Mary cried. "Aren't they pretty?"

"They are—grotesque!" Mrs. Todd said. "Both of you must change your dresses at once."

Lizzie ran from the room. Mary began to cry.

"You are all just mean!" she shouted between sobs. "It's not fair that I can't have pretty clothes!"

"Mary, dear—," Mrs. Todd said. But Mary was deaf to anybody's words but her own. "I won't change my dress!" she cried. She turned and ran out into the garden. The whole family was mean, she thought, and her stepmother was the worst of all.

"My dress is *not* grotesque," she told herself. She looked down at it. Suddenly she saw how crooked the hoops were, and how the dark wood showed through the thin white cloth. She pulled at her skirt to straighten it. It still hung twisted and out of shape. Why, she had been so busy fixing it that she had never really looked at it!

Mary was a quick-tempered girl, but she was also an honest one. "Ma was right," she said aloud. Shame swept over her. How could she make up to her mother for her rudeness?

Suddenly she spied a perfect red rosebud. "Ma loves roses," she thought. She picked the bud. Head high, she marched back to the dining room. Mary went straight to her mother and handed her the rosebud.

Mrs. Todd understood. "Thank you, my little Mary," she said.

Chaney, the cook, came in with a tray of food. "Everybody eat these hotcakes before they are cold-cakes," she ordered.

Mary looked at her mother. "Shall I change after breakfast, ma?" Lizzie had already changed and was at the table.

Mrs. Todd nodded. She pinned the rosebud to her dress. A smile lit Mary's face as she sat down. Ma was going to wear the rose to church! No girl in Lexington could cry harder than Mary Todd. But none had a sunnier smile either.

Chapter *2*

Dinner with Henry Clay

"One—two—three—and turn!" In a loud voice Madame Mentelle counted out the steps for her dancing class. "Keep time to the music, girls. One—two—"

Thirteen-year-old Mary stepped and turned. She liked to dance.

"One—two—three—and curtsy!" said Madame Mentelle. "Very good. That is enough dancing for today. It is time now for your French class."

Mary liked to speak French just as much as she liked to dance. She liked to read too, and to write poetry.

"Mary is smart and quick to learn," her teachers said.

It was no secret that Mary Todd was the best student in Madame Mentelle's school for girls in Lexington.

Mary's father was a rich man, and he saw to it that his children were given the finest training. At home Mary always had good books to read. And there was good conversation.

Mary's tall, quiet father was her hero. He was a businessman and had been a state senator. Like his family before him, he was interested in politics. In the Todd family there had been governors, senators, and judges.

Mr. Todd often talked to Mary about politics. He explained how men were elected to run the government. He told her how important it was to elect wise men. Sometimes he took her with him when he visited political friends. In those days most girls were not interested in politics, but Mary was different. She loved the excitement of meeting famous people.

Many important men visited Lexington. Often Mr. Todd invited them to his big brick home for dinner. When they talked about government matters, Mary listened with sharp ears. Sometimes she joined in.

"Old Andrew Jackson is putting on a lively campaign for reelection to the presidency," a visitor said one day. "When he comes to Lexington there is to be a big picnic for him. Some of the women plan to cook a whole pig."

"There are other men who would make better presidents of the United States," Mr. Todd said.

"Mr. Jackson won't be reelected,"

Mary spoke up suddenly. "He will be snowed under by so many votes for Henry Clay that his long face will freeze. He will never be able to smile again."

The men laughed. But Mrs. Todd shook her head. She did not think it was ladylike to say such things.

Henry Clay was one of Mr. Todd's Lexington friends. He had held many high offices. Mary had known him since she was a baby, and she often visited his beautiful home "Ashland."

"Mr. Henry Clay is the handsomest man in town and has the best manners of anybody—except my father," Mary said.

So when her father gave her a new pony, Mary rode it to Ashland. A servant came to the door. "Mr. and Mrs. Clay have guests," he told her.

"Tell him that Miss Mary Todd is calling," young Mary said grandly.

Soon Mr. Clay came out, a smile on his face.

"I've brought my new pony to dance for you," Mary cried. She raised the reins, and the white pony reared and pawed the air.

Mr. Clay clapped his hands. "What a smart pony!" he said. He lifted Mary from her saddle. "You must join us for dinner."

Seated in the big dining room, Mary almost forgot to eat. She was too busy listening to the men talk politics. At last she could keep quiet no longer.

"Mr. Clay, my father says you will be the next president of the United States," she said. "I wish I could go to Washington and live in the White House. I begged my father to be president, but he only laughed. He said he would rather see you there than be president himself."

"Well," said Henry Clay, "if I am ever president, I shall expect Mary Todd to be one of my first guests."

Mary's cheeks turned pink with pleasure.

"Someday I shall visit the White House!" she thought.

Chapter 3

Happy Young People

The years passed quickly for Mary. Almost before she knew it her schooldays were over. She had gone to school much longer than most girls of her time. After Madame Mentelle's, she had studied for two more years with Dr. John Ward. He was one of the best teachers in Lexington.

When she was 20, Mary visited her sister Elizabeth in Springfield, Illinois. Elizabeth had married Ninian Edwards, son of the governor of Illinois.

Springfield was a small town, but it

was the new capital of the state. There were many political meetings and many parties. After the quiet of Lexington, Mary loved the gay, busy life in Springfield.

"I am going to stay for a long time," she told Elizabeth.

"Good," said Elizabeth.

Mary's cousin John Todd Stuart also lived in Springfield. He had a young law partner named Abraham Lincoln.

Mary first met Abraham Lincoln at a party. She looked very pretty that night. Her blue eyes were shining, and she wore a rose in her soft brown hair.

"Miss Todd, I want to dance with you in the worst way," Abraham Lincoln said.

He did dance with her in the worst way. Awkward Abe stepped all over her slippers!

Abe Lincoln was so tall that Mary came only to his shoulder. He had black hair that would not stay combed and a thin, homely face. But his gray eyes were kind and full of fun. Mary liked him.

After that party, Abraham Lincoln often went to the Edwardses' big house to see Mary. The two found they were interested in many of the same things. They read books together and wrote funny poems. They talked about politics. Mary told him of her home in Kentucky.

"I was born in Kentucky too," he said, "in a log cabin. When I was about six my father put an axe in my hands and set me to work chopping down trees. Everybody had to work hard to get enough to eat. I went to school for only about three months.

Anything else I know I learned by myself from books."

People began to make jokes to Mary about her "tall beau." But Mary had many gentlemen friends. One was Stephen A. Douglas, another lawyer.

"Young Douglas is smart," Ninian told Mary and Elizabeth one evening as they sat at supper. "He is going to be an important man some day."

"So is Mr. Lincoln," Mary said.

Elizabeth looked troubled. "Mary, I wish you were not so friendly with Mr. Lincoln. He is different from you. You grew up in a beautiful home and went to the best schools. He grew up in the backwoods among rough people. He does not even know how to dress or how to act at a party. I don't understand what you see in someone like him."

"I see someone kind and good," Mary said. "He has a fine mind, and he has taught himself."

"He will be a poor man all his life," said rich Ninian.

Mary did not care if Abraham Lincoln was poor. They had good times together. Before long they fell in love.

"I am going to marry Mr. Lincoln," Mary told her sister and brother-in-law.

"Oh, Mary, I can't let you make such a bad mistake," Elizabeth cried.

Mary's eyes flashed angrily. "Do not say one word against him, for I will not listen to you," she told her sister.

Elizabeth and Ninian saw that Mary would not change her mind. So Ninian said, "We will have the wedding here."

It was raining hard in Springfield on the cold, dark night of November 4, 1842. But inside the Edwardses' big house every lamp was lit. Open fires burned brightly. Many of their friends were there to help eat the wedding cake that stood on the dining room table.

Mary looked lovely in a white dress. She was very happy as she and her "tall beau" were married. On her finger Abraham Lincoln placed a gold wedding ring. He had had three words put inside the ring. They were, "Love is eternal."

Chapter 4

The Congressman's Wife

Mary was busy in the kitchen making apple pies. Two small boys played on the floor with a toy wagon. Out in the backyard Abraham Lincoln chopped stove wood. Soon he came into the kitchen with an armload of sticks.

"Is this enough wood to cook pies?" he asked.

"Plenty," Mary said. "Oh, just think how long it will be before I make pies in this kitchen again!"

He grinned. "Are you already sorry

that we are going to Washington, Molly?"

"Of course not, Mr. Lincoln!" Mary said. She called him "Mr. Lincoln," and he called her "Molly." "I am proud that my husband has been elected to Congress. I'll like living in Washington even if I do miss my own kitchen."

Much had happened to Mr. and Mrs. Abraham Lincoln in the five years since they had married. Two sons were born—Bob, now four, and Eddy, who was not yet two. Mr. Lincoln had made such a good name as a lawyer that he had just been elected to the House of Representatives. Soon the family would leave Springfield for the nation's capital.

Several days later the Lincolns started out. They planned to stop on the way for a visit with the Todds in Kentucky. Most of the Todds had never met Abraham Lincoln.

It was a long, hard trip from Springfield to Lexington. It took almost two weeks by stagecoach, by riverboat, and on a noisy little train. In Lexington old Nelson met their train. He was the Todd coachman, and he was wearing his best blue coat with silver buttons.

"My, I'm glad to see you again, Miss Mary!" he said as he led them to the carriage.

In the big Todd house the Lincolns found the family waiting for them.

"Pa! Ma!" Mary cried. "I have brought my husband and sons to show them off to you." Excitement made Mary's blue eyes shine as the Todds welcomed Abraham Lincoln.

She hugged her young stepbrothers

and sisters. There were eight of them now. Emilie was the youngest. The pretty little girl was frightened when she saw so many strangers. The tall man in the black coat frightened her most of all.

"Is he a giant?" she asked.

Abraham Lincoln loved children. He reached down and picked her up. "So this is little sister," he said.

Emilie looked into the giant's friendly face. Suddenly she felt safe in his strong arms. "I'm not afraid of you anymore," she whispered.

Like Emilie, all the Todds were soon good friends with Abraham Lincoln. Mr. and Mrs. Todd invited many people to their home to meet him. Chaney kept the dinner table loaded with chicken and turkey, sweet potatoes, orange cake, and fresh hot bread spread with honey. "No one can cook like Chaney!" Mary said.

One day Mary took her husband to visit her grandmother. Grandmother Parker lived in a large and beautiful house. But nearby, behind a tall fence, stood a row of small ugly buildings that looked like pens. When runaway slaves were caught, they were kept in the pens until their masters came for them.

As the Lincolns sat with Grandmother Parker on her porch, they heard terrible cries coming from the pens. It sounded as though some of the slaves were being whipped. Perhaps their masters were punishing them.

Abraham Lincoln's face grew sad. He told Mary, "Where I lived I never saw slaves when I was young. You grew up among them."

"Yes," Mary said. "Lexington is lovely, but there has always been this dark, dreadful side of life here. I used to see slaves sold in the town square. Poor mothers would weep as their children were sold away from them. Pa was against slavery, yet he owned Nelson and Chaney and Mammy Sally. They were slaves, but they were like part of the family too. I used to wonder when I was a child if they *minded* being slaves!"

Grandmother Parker spoke up. "I have planned to free my slaves. Slavery is wrong."

Abraham Lincoln nodded. "It is a wrong that has come to us from the past. No man should own another man."

"I feel that way too," Mary said.

Soon after visiting Grandmother

Parker the Lincolns went to Washington. There they rented rooms in a boardinghouse. Mary often took the children for walks or to play in a nearby park.

Sometimes Congressman Lincoln joined his family for a walk. One day they were passing the White House. With a grin he stopped and pointed at it. "It is too bad that Henry Clay was never elected president. You didn't get to visit the White House."

"Mr. Clay would have been a good president," Mary said, "but you would be a better one."

"Imagine me being president!" her husband laughed. "No one but you would think of such a thing, Molly."

"You wait and see, Mr. Lincoln," his wife said. "Someday a lot of people will think of it."

Chapter *5*

At Home in Springfield

Mary liked the nation's capital. Still, she was glad when it was time to go home. "Washington and Lexington are lovely," she said, "but Springfield is the best place of all."

Springfield was still a little town. The sidewalks were made of wooden boards, and pigs rolled in the mud and dust of the streets. The Lincolns had a small story-and-a-half brown house on a corner of Eighth and Jackson Streets. Three blocks past their house the farm country began.

They kept a horse and a cow. They got their water from a well in the backyard and wood from a woodpile. Every morning Mary cleaned and filled the oil lamps.

It was a happy home except when little Eddy grew sick and died. Losing him nearly broke the Lincolns' hearts. But in time two more sons were born—Willie and Tad.

Bob, Willie, and Tad were friendly boys. The neighbors' children liked to come to their house. The youngsters played circus in the barn and soldier in the yard. They raced through the house in games of "Chase-Me." Mary and her husband did not mind the noise.

"Let the children have a good time," they said.

Often Abraham Lincoln took a group

of boys to fish in the Sangamon River. Mary would pack their picnic lunches in big baskets.

"*Sangamon* is an Indian word that means plenty to eat," she told them. "So I have made fried chicken and gingerbread and a great big jar of lemonade!"

Mary was always busy. She cooked and cleaned and sewed. She sewed fancy dresses for herself and shirts for Mr. Lincoln. They were beautiful white shirts with many fine ruffles. Mary loved pretty clothes, and she wanted them for her family as well as for herself.

Sometimes as she sat sewing, her husband stretched out on the floor and read aloud to her. He was so tall that the floor was more comfortable for him than a chair. Usually he read political papers. The Lincolns were still interested in government matters.

Mary still liked parties too. On summer Sundays she often invited a hundred friends home after church for "strawberries and ice cream!"

The little brown house did not really have enough room for such parties. The family needed more room too. One day Mary had an idea.

"I'll surprise Mr. Lincoln the next time he goes away," she thought.

Like many lawyers in Springfield, Abraham Lincoln handled law cases in faraway towns. Sometimes he had to be away from home for several months.

One night when he was away, Mary told her boys, "Tomorrow we are going to raise the roof."

"You mean we'll lift it right off the house?" Bob asked.

"We can't," Willie said. "It's nailed on."

"If we don't have a roof, the rain will fall on me," little Tad cried. "I'll get wet."

Mary laughed. "People raise their roofs to make their homes larger. We will add a second story with five bedrooms upstairs, then put a new roof on top. I hope we can finish it before your father comes home."

The workmen came every day for weeks. They sawed and hammered and painted.

Mary made new curtains for the windows. She bought a black couch for the parlor. It was long enough so that her husband could stretch out on it and be comfortable. She shined the floors and had the bedroom furniture moved upstairs. The boys helped her.

But would Abraham Lincoln like what they were doing? Would he think they had spent too much money? Nobody knew.

At last the house was finished, and just in time! About sunset that evening Willie looked out a parlor window.

"Here comes pa!" he shouted.

Mary hurried to the front door. Bob, Willie, and Tad peeked from behind the window curtains. What would pa do?

Down the street walked Abraham Lincoln. Neighbors came out on their porches to watch. They, too, wanted to see what he would do when he saw how his house had changed.

He reached the corner. He looked up at the tall handsome house. Did he see a parlor curtain move? Did he see three laughing boys peeking from the window? If he did, he made no sign. Instead he turned toward the neighbors on their porches. In a loud voice he called, "Excuse me, friends, but I'm Abe Lincoln and I'm looking for my house. I thought it was on this corner. When I went away a few weeks ago, there was only a one-story house here, and this house has two. I think I must be lost."

With a whoop the boys raced to the door.

"You're not lost, pa!" they shouted.

The neighbors were laughing and so was Mary.

"Welcome home, Mr. Lincoln," she cried.

Abraham Lincoln was laughing too as he hurried up the walk. Everybody could see that he liked his house.

Chapter 6

Days to Remember

Bands played. Bells rang. A crowd of 6,000 people filled the town square of Alton, Illinois.

"Hurrah for the Little Giant!" some shouted.

"Hurrah for good Old Abe, the Giant Killer!" others cried.

Mary and Bob stood by a flag-draped speaker's stand.

"My goodness!" Mary exclaimed. "All this noise will drive your father's speech right out of his head."

Bob laughed. He was fifteen now,

and he had come with his mother from Springfield to this political meeting. They had left Willie and Tad back home with neighbors.

Abraham Lincoln sat on the stand beside the man he was running against for the United States Senate. The man was Stephen A. Douglas, Mary's old beau! Mr. Douglas was already a famous Illinois senator. Now he was trying to win reelection. People called him the "Little Giant" because of his small size.

During this 1858 campaign the two candidates had often appeared together at meetings.

They debated a question that was tearing the country apart. "Debate" means to talk over, with each speaker taking a different side of the issue. The South believed in slavery. Much of the North did not. The question was whether new states joining the Union should be slave or free. If the trouble was not soon settled, it could lead to civil war.

So what the candidates said in this campaign was important. Newspapers all over the nation reported the Lincoln-Douglas debates. Today was the last one.

Mr. Douglas spoke first. He was a handsome and well-dressed man. He said the South had always had slaves. He believed in "state's rights." That meant that each new state should decide for itself if it would have slavery.

"Let the people rule!" he cried.

It was a good speech. Mary knew that he had made many in the crowd believe as he did.

She watched with love and pride as her husband rose to speak. His black coat was wrinkled. As usual, his hair had not stayed combed.

"Some people may not think him handsome," she whispered to Bob. "But his heart is as big as his arms are long."

Abraham Lincoln said that slavery was wrong. Even though the South had always had slaves, that did not make slavery right.

"Nobody has a right to do wrong," he said.

He believed that slavery was like a fire. If it were kept from spreading to new states, it would burn itself out in time.

"Did pa win the debate?" Willie and Tad asked when their parents got home.

"We'll know by the votes on election day," Mary answered.

Election day was gray and wet.

"It will be hard for the farmers to get to the voting places," a worried Mary said that morning. "Their wagons will get stuck in the mud." She knew that her husband counted on the votes of the farm people.

"Perhaps the sun will come out and dry the roads," Bob said.

The sun did not come out. All day the skies were dark, and a cold rain fell on Illinois. Douglas was reelected.

Mary refused to be downhearted. "You'll win next time," she told her husband.

He smiled. "You never give up, do you, Mary?" He called her "Mary" now, but she still called him "Mr. Lincoln."

"You'll see, Mr. Lincoln. Even though you lost, you were right in what you said. People will not forget you," Mary said.

It was true. Many people remembered Abraham Lincoln. In 1860 he was chosen to be the Republican candidate for president of the United States. Stephen A. Douglas was a Democratic candidate.

What excitement there was in the Lincolns' house! "Hurrah for Old Abe!" shouted Willie and Tad, now ten and eight.

Suddenly Mary found herself very busy. Many important politicians visited Springfield to see Abraham Lincoln. Newspaper reporters from far away came to write stories about him and his family. Artists arrived to paint his picture.

Mary was up early every morning cleaning her house. She dressed herself and the little boys carefully. Then she baked a yellow cake she called "Election Cake." It was for the visitors and well-wishers who came almost every day. Sometimes by evening guests were seated in every chair in the parlor!

All Springfield was in an uproar. There were speeches and fireworks. There were parades past the Lincoln house.

Mary and the boys watched the parades from the upstairs windows. Bands played. At night the marchers held burning torches. In one parade there were 6,000 people. It took almost three hours for them all to pass the house.

Yet nobody could really be sure

that Abraham Lincoln would be elected president.

Election day came.

Mr. Lincoln spent the day at the State House. Mary stayed at home. It was a worried time for both of them. Waiting for news is hard. By night Mary was very tired.

"Go to bed, Mary," her husband said after supper. "I will stay at the telegraph office. Election news will arrive there. When I learn what has happened, I will come and tell you."

Mary went to bed. It was midnight when Mr. Lincoln came home. He went into the bedroom. By the lamplight he saw Mary sleeping. He touched her shoulder, and she opened her eyes.

"Mary," he said. "Mary, Mary, we are elected!"

Chapter 7

A Divided Nation

A bright sun shone down on the freshly swept streets of Washington. It was March 4, 1861. Abraham Lincoln had just taken office as the sixteenth president of the United States.

A large wooden platform had been built in front of the Capitol for the inauguration. Green-coated men with guns stood on the roofs of nearby buildings. They were there to watch the crowd and to guard the new president.

A proud Mary sat on the platform

with several hundred people. Her husband was making his first speech as president. All she could see of him was the back of his head. But she could hear his voice as he told the crowd that there must be no war. The North and the South must not break apart into two nations.

"We are not enemies, but friends," he said.

Yet Mary knew that war was near. The South still believed that every state had a right to decide for itself if it would have slavery. If states were not allowed this right, Southerners said they would leave the Union. If the North tried to stop them, they would fight. Already some Southern states were raising money for guns and soldiers.

In his speech, Abraham Lincoln

appealed to the people to settle the matter peacefully.

Many of the Todd family had come to see the inauguration. Next morning Mary and the Todd ladies looked over the big White House where the nation's presidents lived. The ladies did not like what they saw.

"Everything is so old and worn," Mary said.

"And dirty!" her sister Elizabeth exclaimed. "Look at the rugs and wallpaper."

The ladies went up the broad stairs and into a bedroom.

"The best thing in this room is the bed. And it is broken from top to bottom!" Elizabeth said.

Mary looked thoughtful. "The White House should be the finest house in the nation," she said.

"Perhaps Congress will give you money to fix things," Elizabeth told her.

Congress did give the First Lady some money. Mary had the windows washed, and the floors shined. She bought beds, chairs, tables, rugs, wallpaper, dishes, and books. She had good taste, and everything she bought was beautiful.

Willie and Tad kept her busy too. They missed their Springfield playmates, and Bob was away studying at Harvard College. Mary learned that two boys lived across the street from the White House—Bud and Holly Taft. She wrote their mother a note inviting the boys over.

Bud was about Willie's age, and Holly was Tad's age. Soon the four were friends and were together often.

The boys ran through the White House shouting and laughing. They wrestled with the president or sat at his knees while he told them a story. They took Tad and Willie's two pet goats and hitched them to a kitchen chair. Then they drove the goats and the chair through the great East Room where White House parties were held.

Down the long room they raced—*clippety-clop*—and back again—*lickety-lop*. The little goats pranced, and the boys shouted, "Gid-dap!" Overhead the glass lamps shook and rattled.

President and Mrs. Lincoln liked to watch the children at play. It made their dark days brighter, for war had come to the nation.

In February, seven of the Southern states had left the Union. They called their new nation the Confederate States of America. Soon the rest of the Southern states joined them. President Lincoln said that the United States could not be split in half. He called for an army of 75,000 Northern troops to fight to save the Union.

Now soldiers were camped on the White House grounds. More army tents stood on the banks of the Potomac River that flowed past Washington. When soldiers marched to the beat of drums, the little boys thought it exciting. But Mary knew it was very sad.

On a hot July morning Mary awoke to the sound of heavy guns.

She ran to a window. Across the river lay the green fields of Virginia, a Southern state. A great battle was going on there. It lasted all day. Mary stood at the window often, trying to see and hear.

People in Washington told one another, "The North will win this battle, and the war will soon be over."

Evening brought them bad news. The North had lost at the Battle of Bull Run. Now everyone knew it might be a long war.

It was believed the South might attack the capital. General Scott told the president that his family should be sent to a safer place.

"Will you go with us?" Mary asked her husband.

He shook his head. "I will not leave Washington at this time."

"Then I will not leave you at this time," Mary said.

The war dragged on. Christmas came. Bob arrived home for a Christmas visit.

"It is wonderful to have the family together again," Mary said.

In the evenings the Lincolns sat around the fireplace. They ate apples and nuts and told Bob all that had happened to them while he was away.

"Bob, you should have seen the big party ma and pa had in honor of Prince Napoleon of France," Tad said. "Napoleon looked grand with a red sash across his chest."

"Pa looked pretty plain in his black suit. But ma was dressed up, you bet," Willie said.

"I'll bet," Bob laughed.

His mother and father laughed too.

It was a good Christmas for the family in the White House.

Chapter 8

The White House

Mary tried to smile as she talked to her guests. But upstairs in the White House, Willie lay sick.

Downstairs the president and his wife were giving a party. They had 500 guests. Some were listening to the music of the Marine Band. Some were eating the fine supper laid out in the state dining room—turkey, duck, ham, fruit. A few were telling Mary how pretty she looked. She had on a new white dress with a long train that lay on the floor behind her.

Before the party, the president had

looked at that train and smiled. "My, what a long tail our cat has tonight!"

Now as the party went on, Mary worried and watched for a chance to slip away from her guests. At last it came. She hurried up the stairs to Willie's room. He was asleep.

Mary felt his hot cheeks and grew more worried. She wished there were no party in the White House tonight. Slowly she went back down the stairs.

In the next days, Willie's fever grew worse. Then Tad became ill with the same kind of fever. Mary sat beside their beds day and night.

One sad morning the doctor told the Lincolns that Willie could not get well. Bob came home from college to be with his family. Only Bob stood beside his heartbroken father in the East Room during Willie's funeral. Tad was

still sick. Mary was in bed, too, ill from grief.

It took a long time for Tad to get well and even longer for Mary. Her family was the most important thing in the world to Mary. Losing dearly loved Willie was almost more than she could bear.

By the time she was well, Bud and Holly Taft had gone away to school. No longer were there four laughing boys to scamper through the White House. Only Tad was left.

With Tad beside her, Mary visited wounded soldiers in the hospitals. She took them lemons and oranges. She always had time to stop at each bed and talk to each lonely soldier. Comforting them helped to comfort her own aching heart.

The soldiers all liked the First Lady.

They saw that she was kind. But there were people who did not like her.

These were political enemies of the president. They hoped to harm him through his wife. From Mary's first days in Washington, they had found fault with her.

"She is a nobody from a country town in the West," they said. "She will not know how to be a First Lady."

Soon they saw that Mary did know how to care for the White House and to give the parties that were part of a president's job. She dressed nicely. She was smart and could discuss politics. She even spoke French with visitors from France.

So they said, "She is too interested in clothes and parties. She spends too much money on the White House. She tries to meddle in political matters. She has a sharp tongue."

They found fault with the president too, especially when he signed the Emancipation Proclamation. This was the famous paper that said the slaves in the South could be free.

Some of the things people said about Mary were true. She did love clothes and parties. And she had spent more money on the White House than Congress had given her. The president said he would pay Mary's extra bills from his own pocket. He knew she had only wanted to make the White House beautiful.

Quick-tempered Mary talked back sharply to those who found fault with her. That made more enemies for the president. Then Mary was sorry, and she tried to make up with the people. Few of them understood that beneath her quick hot words lay a good heart.

Most of the ugly things that people said about Mary were untrue. The worst was that she was a traitor to the North! They knew that her family, the Todds, lived in Kentucky, where many people sided with the South.

"Mary's brothers are fighting for the South," people said. "She wants the South to win."

"Why should I want the rebels to win?" Mary exclaimed fiercely. "They would hang my husband tomorrow if they could."

Some of Mary's brothers did fight for the South. Three of them were killed. Mary had loved them, but she dared not let people see her grief. She could only cry into her pillow at

night. They were the tears of a sister, not a traitor.

Sometimes in the dark nights Mary cried for the president too. The long war had been hard on him. Often he was too busy to eat or rest. He grew very thin and tired. When Mary saw him working at his desk late into the night, she worried about his health. She was also worried for his safety. Once he was shot at when he was riding on horseback to the Soldiers' Home. The bullet went through his tall stovepipe hat.

The war was almost three years old when Mary's "little sister" Emilie visited the White House. It was December 1863.

Emilie did not look like the pretty child who had thought Abraham Lincoln was a giant, nor the lovely girl who had often visited the Lincolns in Springfield. She was pale and sad. Her young husband had just been killed fighting for the South.

Now in the White House the Lincolns hugged the youngest Todd sister. They wanted to comfort her.

"You must stay with us as long as you can, little sister," the president said.

But at once people began to say that the Lincolns had an "enemy" from the South in the White House.

Emilie saw that she was causing trouble. So she said that she must leave. Sadly the president and Mary told her good-bye. She had been with them for only a week.

The terrible war was not only breaking the nation apart. It was breaking families apart too.

Chapter *9*

Assassination!

April sunshine lighted the White House windows. Around the breakfast table sat the president and Mrs. Lincoln, Bob, and Tad.

There was a look of happiness on every face. After four long years the North had won the Civil War. Now the Union was saved and the slaves were free.

Bob was a grown man now. He had just come safely home from the fighting. After finishing college he had joined the army. Mary looked at him proudly and put more eggs on his plate.

"I've brought you a present, pa," Bob said. He held out a little picture of the great Southern general, Robert E. Lee.

The president looked carefully at General Lee's picture.

"It is the face of a noble, brave man," he said. "Soon we shall live in peace with all the brave men who have been fighting us. We can all be cheerful again."

Mary said, "You and I will begin by going to Ford's Theater tonight. There is a funny play."

That night the Lincolns rode in their carriage over the cobblestone streets to the theater. Clouds hid the moon, and the wind was sharp. But Mary felt safe and warm beside her husband. She remembered a talk they'd had earlier in the day.

"After I leave office, I want to take you and Tad to Europe," the president had told her. He still had four more years as president, for he had been elected to a second term. Mary had not seen her husband so happy in a long time.

"Everything is going to be better from now on," she thought as they drew up in front of the theater.

Inside the theater people stood and clapped for the president. The Lincolns took their seats in a flag-draped box at one side of the stage.

The theater lights were dimmed. On the stage the actors began to speak their lines. Soon the audience was laughing.

In their dark box, the president

reached out and took Mary's hand. So they sat, holding hands and laughing. They did not hear a man creep into the back of the box.

Suddenly a shot rang out. The president fell forward in his chair, a great wound in the back of his head. The gunman jumped down on the stage and ran off.

For a moment Mary did not know what had happened. Then she screamed, "The president is shot!"

After that, everything was noise and confusion in Ford's Theater. Men carried the president to a bedroom in a house across the street. He was too badly wounded for the long trip back to the White House. People said that the gunman had been John Wilkes Booth, a crazed Southern actor.

For the rest of the night, Mary sat

in the little parlor of the borrowed house. Friends came to be with her. Bob came and stood beside his father's bed. Doctors came—sixteen in all. They did what they could for the president, but they knew he could not be saved. Vice President Andrew Johnson came. Tomorrow he would be the new president.

At times through the night, Mary went to her husband's bedside. It was a small wooden bed and too short for the president. His feet hung over the side. He did not look wounded. He looked as if he were sleeping. Mary kneeled beside him and wept.

In the morning, rain beat against the parlor windows.

Bob came to Mary. "Pa is gone," he said.

He led her to Abraham Lincoln's

side. A wild grief swept over Mary. She threw herself across her husband's body.

"Oh, why did you not tell me he was dying!" she cried.

Bob took his mother outside to a waiting carriage. Church bells were tolling. It was raining hard, as though the sky itself wept on that morning of April 15, 1865.

Mary looked across the street at the dark brick front of Ford's Theater. "Oh, that dreadful house! That dreadful house!" she said.

After Abraham Lincoln's funeral, a grieving Mary and her sons left the White House and moved to Chicago. Mary never lived in Washington again. She missed her husband too much. She knew that in Washington she would feel even sadder without him.

For a long while she and Tad traveled in Europe, just as Mr. Lincoln had planned they should all do together. Then when Tad was eighteen, he died of a lung disease. To Mary, this was the final blow. Her health failed, and for many years she was ill.

Mary never got over the loss of her husband. But as time went by she did find some happiness in the way the nation loved and honored his memory.

Finally Mary went back to Springfield to live with her sister Elizabeth.

On a golden summer evening she died in that same house where she and Abraham Lincoln had been married so many years before. She was 63. On her finger she still wore the ring that said, "Love is eternal."